Table Of Contents

Chapter 1: Introduction to Digital Marketing

Understanding the Basics of Digital Marketing

In today's digital age, where technology has become an integral part of our lives, it is crucial for small business owners to grasp the basics of digital marketing. With the ever-increasing reliance on the internet, understanding digital marketing has become essential to reach and engage with potential customers effectively. This subchapter aims to provide a practical guide to small business owners, covering various aspects of digital marketing that will help them thrive in the competitive online landscape.

Digital marketing is a broad term that encompasses several niche areas, including social media marketing, search engine optimization (SEO), content marketing, mobile marketing, video marketing, and conversion rate optimization. Each of these areas plays a significant role in creating a successful digital marketing strategy.

Social media marketing is all about using platforms such as Facebook, Instagram, Twitter, and LinkedIn to connect with your target audience, build brand awareness, and drive traffic to your website. It involves creating engaging content, running targeted ads, and leveraging analytics to measure your results.

Search engine optimization (SEO) focuses on optimizing your website to rank higher in search engine results. By using relevant keywords, optimizing your website's structure, and building quality backlinks, you can improve your website's visibility and attract organic traffic.

Content marketing revolves around creating and distributing valuable and relevant content to attract and retain a clearly defined audience. This could be in the form of blog posts, e-books, videos, or podcasts. By providing valuable information to your audience, you can establish yourself as an industry expert and build trust with potential customers.

Mobile marketing is all about reaching and engaging with your audience on their mobile devices. With the increasing use of smartphones, it is crucial to optimize your website and marketing campaigns for mobile users to ensure a seamless user experience.

Video marketing has gained immense popularity in recent years, with platforms like YouTube and TikTok becoming major marketing channels. By creating engaging and informative videos, you can capture your audience's attention and communicate your brand message effectively.

Conversion rate optimization focuses on turning website visitors into paying customers. By analyzing user behavior, conducting A/B tests, and optimizing your website's design and content, you can improve your conversion rates and maximize your return on investment.

In conclusion, understanding the basics of digital marketing is essential for small business owners in today's digital age. By grasping the concepts of social media marketing, SEO, content marketing, mobile marketing, video marketing, and conversion rate optimization, small business owners can effectively reach and engage with their target audience, drive traffic to their website, and ultimately achieve their business goals.

Benefits of Digital Marketing for Small Businesses

In today's digital age, small businesses have the opportunity to level the playing field with larger corporations through the power of digital marketing. With the right strategies and tools, small business owners can effectively reach their target audience, boost their online presence, and increase their sales and revenue. In this subchapter, we will explore the numerous benefits that digital marketing offers to small businesses across various niches, including digital marketing, social media marketing, search engine optimization (SEO), content marketing, mobile marketing, video marketing, and conversion rate optimization.

Digital marketing, as a whole, provides small businesses with a cost-effective method to promote their products or services and compete with larger competitors. Compared to traditional marketing channels, digital marketing allows for precise targeting and measurable results, ensuring that every penny spent on marketing efforts is maximized.

Social media marketing has become an essential aspect of digital marketing, enabling small businesses to connect and engage with their target audience on platforms like Facebook, Instagram, Twitter, and LinkedIn. Through strategic social media campaigns, small business owners can build brand awareness, drive website traffic, and ultimately increase conversions and sales.

Search engine optimization (SEO) is crucial for small businesses to improve their visibility in search engine results and increase organic traffic to their websites. By optimizing their website's content, structure, and user experience, small businesses can rank higher in search engine results and attract highly targeted traffic.

Content marketing plays a vital role in establishing thought leadership and building trust with customers. By creating and distributing valuable and relevant content, small businesses can position themselves as industry experts and gain the trust of their target audience, leading to increased brand loyalty and customer retention.

Mobile marketing has become increasingly important as more consumers use their smartphones to browse the internet and make purchases. Small businesses can leverage mobile marketing techniques such as mobile-friendly websites, SMS marketing, and mobile apps to reach their audience on the go, driving engagement and conversions.

Video marketing has emerged as a powerful tool for small businesses to convey their brand message and engage with their target audience. By creating compelling video content, small businesses can increase brand awareness, showcase their products or services, and foster a deeper connection with their customers.

Conversion rate optimization focuses on improving the effectiveness of a small business's website and landing pages to convert visitors into customers. By analyzing user behavior, conducting A/B tests, and making data-driven changes, small businesses can optimize their website's conversion rate, leading to increased sales and revenue.

In conclusion, digital marketing offers a myriad of benefits for small businesses across various niches. By leveraging digital marketing strategies such as social media marketing, SEO, content marketing, mobile marketing, video marketing, and conversion rate optimization, small business owners can level the playing field, reach their target audience, and achieve their business goals in a cost-effective and measurable way.

Chapter 2: Developing a Digital Marketing Strategy

Setting Clear Goals and Objectives

As a small business owner venturing into the world of digital marketing, it is crucial to set clear goals and objectives to ensure the success of your online efforts. Without a clear direction, your digital marketing strategies may lack focus and fail to deliver the desired results. In this subchapter, we will explore the importance of setting clear goals and objectives for various aspects of digital marketing, including social media marketing, search engine optimization (SEO), content marketing, mobile marketing, video marketing, and conversion rate optimization.

Setting goals and objectives helps to provide a roadmap for your digital marketing campaigns. It allows you to define what you want to achieve and enables you to measure the success of your efforts. For instance, if your goal is to increase brand awareness through social media marketing, you can set objectives such as increasing the number of followers, improving engagement rates, or driving more traffic to your website through social media channels. By clearly defining these goals and objectives, you can track your progress and make adjustments along the way.

When it comes to search engine optimization (SEO), setting clear goals and objectives is essential. You may aim to improve your website's search engine rankings, increase organic traffic, or generate more leads through SEO efforts. By setting specific targets, you can focus on optimizing your website's content, improving technical aspects, and implementing effective link-building strategies.

Content marketing goals often revolve around creating valuable and engaging content to attract and retain customers. You can set objectives such as increasing blog subscribers, generating more leads through content downloads, or improving content engagement metrics. By setting clear goals, you can tailor your content strategy to meet the needs of your audience and measure its effectiveness.

Mobile marketing plays a significant role in reaching consumers on their smartphones and tablets. Setting goals and objectives in this area can include increasing mobile app downloads, improving mobile website conversions, or enhancing user experience on mobile devices. Clear objectives will guide your mobile marketing efforts and ensure you stay ahead in today's mobile-driven world.

Video marketing can be a powerful tool for small businesses. Setting goals and objectives for video marketing could involve increasing video views, improving engagement rates, or driving more conversions through video content. By setting clear targets, you can create compelling videos that resonate with your target audience and achieve your desired outcomes.

Conversion rate optimization focuses on improving your website's ability to convert visitors into customers. Setting clear goals and objectives for conversion rate optimization can involve increasing website conversions, reducing bounce rates, or improving user experience. By setting specific targets, you can identify areas for improvement and implement strategies to optimize your website's conversion funnel.

In conclusion, setting clear goals and objectives is crucial for small business owners diving into the world of digital marketing. Whether it's social media marketing, SEO, content marketing, mobile marketing, video marketing, or conversion rate optimization, clearly defining your goals will help you stay focused, measure your progress, and achieve success in your digital marketing endeavors.

Identifying Target Audience and Buyer Persona

In today's digital age, understanding your target audience and crafting a buyer persona is crucial for the success of your small business. In this subchapter, we will delve into the importance of identifying your target audience and creating buyer personas to guide your digital marketing strategies across various niches, including digital marketing, social media marketing, search engine optimization (SEO), content marketing, mobile marketing, video marketing, and conversion rate optimization.

Your target audience is the group of people who are most likely to be interested in your products or services. By identifying and understanding your target audience, you can tailor your marketing efforts to reach the right people at the right time, increasing your chances of converting them into paying customers.

To start, you need to conduct thorough market research. This involves collecting data and insights about your industry, competitors, and potential customers. Utilize online tools, surveys, and interviews to gather information about your target audience's demographics, interests, pain points, and purchasing behavior.

Once you have gathered this data, it's time to create buyer personas. A buyer persona is a fictional representation of your ideal customer. It helps you understand their needs, motivations, and behaviors, allowing you to tailor your marketing messages accordingly.

Begin by giving your buyer persona a name and detailing their demographics, such as age, gender, location, and occupation. Dive deeper into their interests, hobbies, and values. Identify their pain points and challenges that your product or service can address. Consider their preferred communication channels and the devices they use, as this will guide your digital marketing efforts.

Having a clear understanding of your target audience and buyer personas will enable you to develop effective digital marketing strategies. For instance, in social media marketing, you can focus your efforts on platforms where your target audience is most active. In SEO, you can optimize your website and content to target specific keywords that resonate with your audience. In content marketing, you can create valuable and relevant content that addresses their pain points and positions your business as a trusted authority.

Furthermore, mobile marketing and video marketing can be leveraged to capture the attention of your target audience, who are increasingly consuming content on their mobile devices. Lastly, conversion rate optimization techniques can be implemented to enhance the user experience and increase the likelihood of converting visitors into customers.

In conclusion, understanding your target audience and creating buyer personas is essential for small business owners in the digital marketing landscape. By identifying your target audience's demographics, interests, pain points, and preferences, you can tailor your marketing strategies to effectively reach and engage them. This subchapter will equip you with the knowledge and tools necessary to identify your target audience and create buyer personas that will drive the success of your digital marketing efforts.

Competitor Analysis

In the fast-paced world of digital marketing, staying ahead of the competition is crucial for small business owners. To thrive in the digital landscape, it is essential to understand your competitors and their strategies. This subchapter will guide you through the process of conducting a comprehensive competitor analysis, helping you gain valuable insights and develop effective strategies to outperform your rivals.

Digital Marketing: Competitor analysis in digital marketing involves analyzing your competitors' online presence, including their website, social media profiles, and digital advertising campaigns. By assessing their digital marketing tactics, you can identify areas where they excel and learn from their successes, while also uncovering weaknesses that you can exploit to gain a competitive edge.

Social Media Marketing: Analyzing your competitors' social media presence is vital in understanding their target audience, engagement strategies, and content tactics. By monitoring their social media channels, you can identify the platforms they are active on, the type of content that resonates with their audience, and the frequency and timing of their posts. Armed with this knowledge, you can refine your own social media strategy to reach and engage your target audience more effectively.

Search Engine Optimization (SEO): Competitor analysis in SEO involves identifying the keywords your competitors are targeting and assessing their website's search engine rankings. By understanding the keywords they rank for, you can optimize your own website's content to target high-value keywords that drive relevant traffic. Additionally, analyzing their backlink profile can help you identify potential link-building opportunities to improve your own website's authority and visibility in search results.

Content Marketing: Analyzing your competitors' content marketing efforts can provide insights into the type of content that resonates with your target audience. By assessing their content strategy, you can identify gaps in the market and create unique, valuable content that sets your business apart. Additionally, monitoring their content distribution channels can help you identify platforms where you can promote your content and reach a wider audience.

Mobile Marketing: Understanding how your competitors engage with their mobile audience can help you optimize your own mobile marketing strategies. By evaluating their mobile apps, mobile advertising campaigns, and mobile website design, you can identify opportunities to enhance user experience and increase customer engagement on mobile devices.

Video Marketing: Analyzing your competitors' video marketing strategies can help you identify effective storytelling techniques, video formats, and distribution channels. By understanding their video content's strengths and weaknesses, you can create compelling videos that resonate with your target audience and differentiate your brand.

Conversion Rate Optimization: Analyzing your competitors' conversion strategies can help you identify best practices and areas for improvement in your own conversion funnel. By assessing their website design, landing pages, calls-to-action, and user experience, you can optimize your own conversion process to increase conversions and drive more revenue.

In conclusion, conducting a thorough competitor analysis across various digital marketing channels is essential for small business owners to stay competitive in the digital landscape. By gaining insights into your competitors' strategies, you can refine your own marketing efforts, differentiate your brand, and ultimately achieve greater success in your niche.

Budgeting and Allocating Resources

In the fast-paced digital world, small business owners need to have a clear understanding of budgeting and allocating resources for their digital marketing efforts. This subchapter aims to provide practical guidance on how to effectively manage finances and allocate resources for various digital marketing activities such as social media marketing, search engine optimization (SEO), content marketing, mobile marketing, video marketing, and conversion rate optimization.

One of the key aspects of budgeting for digital marketing is setting clear goals and objectives. Small business owners should outline their marketing goals and align them with their overall business objectives. This will help in determining the budget required for each digital marketing niche. For instance, if the goal is to increase brand awareness through social media marketing, a dedicated budget must be allocated to creating engaging content and running targeted ad campaigns on platforms like Facebook, Instagram, and Twitter.

Search engine optimization (SEO) is another crucial aspect of digital marketing. Allocating resources for SEO activities involves investing in keyword research, on-page optimization, link building, and monitoring website analytics. Budgeting for SEO should also consider the cost of hiring an SEO expert or outsourcing SEO services to ensure the best results.

Content marketing plays a vital role in building a brand's online presence. Allocating resources for content creation, distribution, and promotion is crucial for attracting and engaging potential customers. This could include investing in professional copywriters, graphic designers, and tools for content creation and distribution.

Mobile marketing is gaining significant importance in today's digital landscape. Small business owners should allocate resources for mobile-friendly website design, mobile advertising campaigns, and mobile app development, if applicable.

Video marketing is a highly effective way to engage with audiences. Allocating resources for video creation, production, and promotion can significantly enhance a brand's visibility and engagement. This may involve investing in video equipment, hiring videographers, and leveraging video hosting and distribution platforms.

Conversion rate optimization (CRO) focuses on improving the website's performance in converting visitors into customers. Allocating resources for CRO involves conducting A/B testing, usability testing, and investing in tools and technologies that can help optimize the website's conversion funnel.

In conclusion, budgeting and allocating resources for digital marketing activities require careful planning and consideration. Small business owners must align their marketing goals with their overall business objectives and allocate budgets accordingly. By strategically investing in social media marketing, SEO, content marketing, mobile marketing, video marketing, and conversion rate optimization, small businesses can maximize their digital marketing efforts and achieve significant growth in today's competitive digital landscape.

Chapter 3: Social Media Marketing

Choosing the Right Social Media Platforms

In today's digital age, social media has become an essential tool for small business owners to reach and engage with their target audience. However, with the plethora of social media platforms available, it can be overwhelming to determine which ones are the most effective for your business. This subchapter will guide you through the process of choosing the right social media platforms to maximize your digital marketing efforts.

When selecting the ideal social media platforms for your small business, it is crucial to consider your target audience and their preferences. Each platform caters to a unique demographic, so understanding your audience's characteristics is essential. For instance, if you are targeting a younger demographic, platforms like Instagram and Snapchat might be more suitable, while LinkedIn may be better for a professional audience.

Furthermore, it is important to align your social media strategy with your overall marketing goals. Consider the type of content you want to create and the objectives you want to achieve. Are you looking to increase brand awareness, generate leads, or drive website traffic? Different platforms offer varying features and opportunities, so selecting the ones that align with your goals will ensure you make the most of your digital marketing efforts.

Another factor to consider is the resources and capabilities of your small business. Managing multiple social media platforms can be time-consuming, and it is vital to realistically assess your capacity. It is better to focus on a few platforms and do them well, rather than spreading yourself too thin and delivering subpar results across various channels. Choose platforms that you can consistently maintain and engage with to build a strong online presence.

Additionally, staying updated with the latest trends and changes in social media platforms is crucial. The digital landscape is ever-evolving, and what works today may not be as effective tomorrow. Stay informed about new features, algorithm updates, and emerging platforms to ensure your small business remains competitive in the digital marketing arena.

In conclusion, choosing the right social media platforms for your small business requires careful consideration of your target audience, marketing goals, available resources, and staying updated with industry trends. By selecting the platforms that align with your objectives and effectively reaching your target audience, you can leverage social media to boost your digital marketing, enhance brand presence, and drive business growth.

Creating Engaging Social Media Content

In this subchapter, we will explore the importance of creating engaging social media content and how it can benefit small business owners. In today's digital age, social media plays a crucial role in the success of any marketing strategy. With millions of active users on various platforms, it has become a hub for businesses to connect with their target audience, build brand awareness, and drive sales. However, simply having a presence on social media is not enough. To stand out in the crowded digital landscape, small business owners need to create engaging content that captivates their audience and encourages them to take action.

Engaging social media content is all about providing value to your audience while also being entertaining and informative. It should resonate with your target market, evoke emotions, and spark conversations. To achieve this, consider the following tips:

1. Know your audience: Understanding your target market is essential in creating content that resonates with them. Conduct market research, develop buyer personas, and identify their pain points, interests, and preferences.

2. Be visual: Visual content is highly engaging on social media platforms. Incorporate eye-catching images, videos, infographics, and memes into your content strategy to grab attention and increase shares.

3. Tell stories: Humans are wired for storytelling. Craft compelling narratives that connect with your audience on an emotional level. Share success stories, behind-the-scenes glimpses, and user-generated content to foster a sense of community and authenticity.

4. Encourage interaction: Social media is all about creating a two-way conversation. Encourage your audience to like, comment, and share your content. Ask questions, run polls, and respond promptly to user comments to foster engagement.

5. Stay consistent: Consistency is key to maintaining a strong social media presence. Develop a content calendar and schedule regular posts to keep your audience engaged. Experiment with different content formats and analyze metrics to determine what works best for your niche.

Remember, creating engaging social media content is an ongoing process. Stay up to date with the latest trends, monitor your analytics, and adapt your strategy accordingly. By consistently producing valuable and captivating content, you can leverage the power of social media to drive traffic, generate leads, and ultimately grow your small business.

Building and Managing Social Media Communities

In today's digital landscape, social media has become an integral part of any successful marketing strategy. As a small business owner, it is crucial to understand the power of social media communities and how to effectively build and manage them. This subchapter will provide you with practical insights and strategies to help you harness the potential of social media marketing for your business.

To begin with, building a social media community requires a clear understanding of your target audience. Identify the platforms where your audience is most active and tailor your efforts accordingly. Whether it's Facebook, Twitter, Instagram, or LinkedIn, each platform has its unique audience and engagement dynamics. By focusing on the platforms that resonate with your target audience, you can establish a strong presence and attract the right followers.

Once you've chosen the appropriate platforms, it's time to create valuable and engaging content. Quality content is the fuel that drives social media communities. Develop a content strategy that aligns with your business goals and audience interests. Consistency is key, so ensure that you regularly share informative, entertaining, and shareable content that reflects your brand's voice and values.

In addition to creating content, actively engage with your community. Respond to comments, messages, and mentions in a timely and personal manner. Encourage discussions, ask questions, and seek feedback. By fostering two-way communication, you can build trust, loyalty, and a sense of community among your followers.

Don't overlook the power of influencers in growing your social media community. Collaborate with influencers in your niche who have a significant following and engage with your target audience. Their authentic endorsement and exposure can help you reach a wider audience and gain credibility within your industry.

Monitoring and analyzing the performance of your social media efforts is vital for ongoing success. Utilize analytics tools to track key metrics such as reach, engagement, and conversions. This data will provide insights into what's working and what's not, allowing you to optimize your strategies and improve results.

Lastly, never underestimate the importance of staying up to date with the latest trends and best practices in social media marketing. The digital landscape is constantly evolving, and what works today may not work tomorrow. Continuously educate yourself through courses, webinars, and industry blogs to stay ahead of the curve and adapt your strategies accordingly.

By building and managing social media communities effectively, small business owners can leverage the power of digital marketing, social media marketing, search engine optimization (SEO), content marketing, mobile marketing, video marketing, and conversion rate optimization to drive brand awareness, engagement, and ultimately, business growth. Embrace these strategies, connect with your audience, and watch your social media communities flourish.

Measuring Social Media ROI

In the fast-paced world of digital marketing, social media has become an indispensable tool for small business owners. However, the key question that often arises is, "How can we measure the return on investment (ROI) of our social media efforts?" After all, as a small business owner, you want to ensure that every penny and minute invested in social media marketing is yielding tangible results.

Measuring social media ROI goes beyond simply tracking the number of likes, shares, or followers your business has acquired. Instead, it requires a more comprehensive approach that takes into account various metrics and factors. Here are some practical tips to help you measure the ROI of your social media efforts effectively:

1. Set clear goals: Before diving into any social media campaign, it's crucial to define your objectives. Whether it's to increase brand awareness, drive website traffic, generate leads, or boost sales, clearly outlining your goals will allow you to measure success more accurately.

2. Track engagement metrics: Monitoring likes, comments, shares, and click-through rates will provide valuable insights into how your audience is interacting with your content. Analyze these metrics regularly to identify patterns and adjust your strategy accordingly.

3. Measure website traffic: Use tools like Google Analytics to track the number of visitors coming to your website from social media platforms. By analyzing the traffic sources, you can determine which social media channels are driving the most valuable traffic.

4. Calculate conversion rates: Conversion tracking allows you to measure the number of leads or sales generated directly from social media. By attributing conversions to specific social media campaigns, you can determine which strategies are most effective in driving conversions.

5. Monitor customer sentiment: Pay attention to the sentiment surrounding your brand on social media. Positive mentions and reviews can indicate successful engagement, while negative feedback may require immediate attention to protect your brand's reputation.

6. Compare costs and revenue: Calculate the costs associated with your social media efforts, including content creation, advertising, and management tools. Compare these costs to the revenue generated through social media channels to determine your overall ROI.

Remember, social media ROI is not a one-size-fits-all metric. The effectiveness of your social media campaigns may vary depending on your industry, target audience, and specific goals. Regularly reviewing and analyzing your social media metrics will allow you to make data-driven decisions, optimize your strategies, and maximize your ROI.

By measuring social media ROI, small business owners like you can gain valuable insights into the impact of your digital marketing efforts. This knowledge will empower you to refine your strategies, enhance engagement with your target audience, and ultimately drive growth for your business.

Chapter 4: Search Engine Optimization (SEO)

Importance of SEO for Small Business Websites

Title: Importance of SEO for Small Business Websites

Introduction:
In today's digital era, having a strong online presence is crucial for small businesses to thrive and compete in their respective industries. One of the most effective ways to boost your visibility and reach a wider audience is through search engine optimization (SEO). This subchapter delves into the importance of SEO for small business websites, providing valuable insights and practical tips to help you navigate the digital marketing landscape successfully.

1. Enhancing Visibility and Organic Traffic:
SEO plays a pivotal role in improving your website's visibility on search engine results pages (SERPs). By optimizing your website's content, keywords, and meta tags, you increase the chances of ranking higher on search engine result pages, making it easier for potential customers to find you. This increased visibility leads to higher organic traffic, ensuring a steady stream of qualified leads for your business.

2. Building Trust and Credibility:
When your website ranks higher on search engines, it instills a sense of trust and credibility among users. People tend to trust websites that appear on the first page of search results, as they perceive them to be more reputable and reliable. Implementing proper SEO techniques, such as creating high-quality content and optimizing user experience, helps establish your small business as a trusted authority in your niche.

3. Cost-Effective Marketing Strategy:
Compared to traditional marketing methods, SEO is a highly cost-effective strategy for small businesses. While it does require an initial investment in terms of time and resources, the long-term benefits outweigh the costs. Unlike paid advertising, SEO generates organic traffic, ensuring a consistent flow of potential customers without ongoing expenses.

4. Targeting the Right Audience:
SEO allows you to target specific keywords and phrases relevant to your industry, ensuring that your website appears in front of the right audience. By optimizing your content and meta tags to align with your target customers' search intent, you attract highly qualified leads who are more likely to convert into paying customers.

5. Staying Ahead of Competitors:
In today's competitive business landscape, staying ahead of the competition is essential. Implementing effective SEO strategies allows you to outperform your competitors in search rankings, gaining a competitive edge. By consistently monitoring and adapting your SEO efforts, you can adapt to changing trends and consumer behavior, ensuring your small business remains relevant and visible.

Conclusion:
In the digital marketing realm, SEO is not just a buzzword; it is an essential tool for small business owners to thrive and succeed. By investing time and effort into optimizing your website for search engines, you can enhance your online visibility, build trust with your audience, and drive targeted traffic to your small business website. Embracing SEO as part of your overall marketing strategy is a wise decision that can yield significant long-term benefits.

Keyword Research and Optimization

In today's digital age, having a strong online presence is crucial for small business owners to succeed. Whether you're a seasoned entrepreneur or just starting out, understanding the importance of keyword research and optimization is key to driving organic traffic and boosting your online visibility. This subchapter will delve into the world of keyword research and optimization, providing practical insights and strategies to help you make the most out of your digital marketing efforts.

Keyword research is the foundation of any successful digital marketing campaign. It involves identifying the words and phrases that your target audience is using to search for products or services like yours. By understanding these keywords, you can optimize your website, social media content, and other marketing materials to rank higher in search engine results pages (SERPs).

To begin your keyword research, put yourself in your customers' shoes. Think about what they would type into a search engine when looking for your business. Use online tools like Google Keyword Planner, Moz Keyword Explorer, or SEMrush to discover relevant keywords and phrases with high search volumes and low competition. These tools provide valuable insights into search trends and help you narrow down your focus.

Once you have a list of keywords, strategically incorporate them into your website's content, meta tags, URLs, and headings. However, it's important to strike a balance between optimization and user experience. Your content should be informative, engaging, and valuable to your audience. Avoid keyword stuffing, as search engines penalize websites that engage in this practice.

In addition to optimizing your website, keyword research can also inform your content marketing strategy. By creating high-quality blog posts, articles, and videos that revolve around popular keywords, you can attract and engage your target audience. This not only establishes you as an industry expert but also increases your chances of ranking higher in search engine results.

Furthermore, keyword research can guide your social media marketing efforts. By incorporating relevant keywords into your social media posts, you can increase your visibility and reach on platforms like Facebook, Instagram, and Twitter. This helps you connect with potential customers who are actively seeking products or services like yours.

In conclusion, keyword research and optimization are essential components of a successful digital marketing strategy for small business owners. By understanding the keywords your target audience uses and strategically incorporating them into your website, content, and social media posts, you can improve your online visibility and attract more qualified leads. Stay tuned for the next chapter, where we'll explore the power of search engine optimization (SEO) in further detail.

On-Page SEO Techniques

In today's digital landscape, having a strong online presence is crucial for small business owners to thrive and compete in the market. One of the most effective ways to boost your visibility and drive traffic to your website is through search engine optimization (SEO). Specifically, on-page SEO techniques play a vital role in enhancing your website's search engine rankings and attracting potential customers. In this subchapter, we will explore various on-page SEO techniques that small business owners can implement to improve their online visibility and drive organic traffic.

First and foremost, optimizing your website's content is essential. This involves conducting thorough keyword research to identify the key terms and phrases that your target audience is searching for. By strategically incorporating these keywords into your website's content, meta tags, headlines, and URLs, you can increase your website's relevance to search engines and improve your chances of appearing in relevant search results.

Additionally, small business owners should focus on optimizing their website's structure and navigation. By ensuring that your website is user-friendly, easy to navigate, and loads quickly, you create a positive user experience that search engines value. This can be achieved by organizing your content into logical categories, using descriptive URLs, and optimizing image file sizes.

Furthermore, leveraging internal linking is another effective on-page SEO technique. By linking relevant pages and posts within your website, you not only improve user experience but also help search engines understand the structure and hierarchy of your website. This can enhance your website's visibility and improve its chances of ranking higher in search engine results.

Incorporating rich and engaging multimedia content, such as videos and infographics, can also boost your on-page SEO efforts. Search engines favor websites that offer valuable and diverse content to users. By integrating multimedia elements into your website, you can increase user engagement, dwell time, and ultimately improve your website's search engine rankings.

Lastly, optimizing your website for mobile devices is crucial in today's mobile-driven world. With a significant portion of online traffic coming from mobile devices, small business owners must ensure that their websites are mobile-responsive and provide a seamless browsing experience across different devices. This not only enhances user experience but also improves your website's chances of ranking higher in mobile search results.

In conclusion, on-page SEO techniques play a vital role in improving your website's visibility and driving organic traffic. By implementing these techniques, small business owners can increase their online presence, reach their target audience more effectively, and ultimately grow their business in the digital age.

Off-Page SEO Techniques

In today's digital landscape, having a strong online presence is crucial for small businesses to thrive. While on-page SEO techniques focus on optimizing your website's content and structure, off-page SEO techniques play an equally important role in boosting your search engine rankings and driving more organic traffic to your website.

Off-page SEO refers to all the activities you perform outside of your website to improve its visibility and credibility in the eyes of search engines like Google. By implementing these techniques, you can enhance your online reputation, build quality backlinks, and establish your business as an authority in your niche.

One of the most effective off-page SEO techniques is link building. By acquiring high-quality backlinks from reputable websites, search engines perceive your website as more trustworthy and relevant, consequently boosting your rankings. You can achieve this by guest blogging on industry-related websites, reaching out to influencers for collaborations, or leveraging business partnerships.

Social media marketing also plays a significant role in off-page SEO. Engaging with your target audience on platforms like Facebook, Instagram, and Twitter not only helps build brand awareness but also increases the chances of your content being shared and linked to. Sharing valuable, shareable content and actively participating in relevant online communities can significantly improve your off-page SEO efforts.

Additionally, content marketing can strengthen your off-page SEO strategy. Creating and distributing high-quality, informative content such as blog posts, articles, and infographics not only helps attract organic traffic but also increases the likelihood of other websites linking back to your content. This not only improves your website's visibility but also establishes your business as an industry thought leader.

Mobile marketing and video marketing are also essential components of off-page SEO. With the rise of mobile devices and video consumption, optimizing your website and content for mobile users and producing engaging videos can significantly boost your search engine rankings and user engagement.

Lastly, conversion rate optimization (CRO) is crucial for enhancing your website's performance and increasing conversions. By analyzing user behavior, conducting A/B testing, and making data-driven optimizations, you can improve your website's user experience, ultimately leading to higher conversions and improved search engine rankings.

In conclusion, off-page SEO techniques are essential for small business owners looking to improve their online visibility and drive organic traffic. By implementing link building strategies, leveraging social media and content marketing, optimizing for mobile and video, and focusing on CRO, you can enhance your website's authority, credibility, and search engine rankings. Stay tuned for the next chapter, where we will dive deeper into on-page SEO techniques to further optimize your website for success in the digital marketing landscape.

Monitoring and Improving SEO Performance

In today's digital landscape, having a strong online presence is crucial for small businesses to thrive. One of the key components of a successful online strategy is search engine optimization (SEO). SEO ensures that your website ranks higher in search engine results, making it easier for potential customers to find you. However, simply implementing SEO techniques is not enough; monitoring and improving your SEO performance is equally important.

Monitoring your SEO performance allows you to assess the effectiveness of your strategies and identify areas for improvement. It helps you understand how your website is performing in search engine rankings and whether your efforts are generating the desired results. By keeping a close eye on your SEO performance, you can make data-driven decisions and optimize your digital marketing efforts accordingly.

There are several tools available to help you monitor your SEO performance. Google Analytics is a popular choice among small business owners as it provides valuable insights about your website's traffic, user behavior, and conversion rates. Additionally, Google Search Console allows you to track your website's visibility in search results and identify any errors or issues that may be affecting your SEO performance.

Improving your SEO performance involves continuous effort and staying up-to-date with the latest trends and best practices. Regularly updating your website with fresh and relevant content is crucial. Content marketing plays a significant role in SEO, as search engines prioritize websites that consistently provide valuable information to users. Incorporating keywords strategically within your content, meta tags, and URLs can also boost your SEO performance.

Social media marketing is another essential aspect of improving SEO performance. Engaging with your audience on platforms like Facebook, Instagram, and Twitter can increase brand visibility and drive traffic to your website. Sharing your content on social media can also generate backlinks, which are crucial for improving your website's authority and search engine rankings.

Mobile marketing and video marketing are two rapidly growing niches that can significantly impact your SEO performance. With the increasing use of smartphones, optimizing your website for mobile devices is essential. Creating mobile-friendly content, ensuring fast loading times, and implementing responsive design are some key factors to consider. Similarly, incorporating video content on your website can enhance user experience and increase engagement, positively impacting your SEO performance.

Conversion rate optimization (CRO) is the final piece of the puzzle. While driving traffic to your website is crucial, converting that traffic into paying customers is equally important. Optimizing your website's design, improving call-to-action buttons, and conducting A/B testing can help increase your conversion rates and maximize the return on your digital marketing efforts.

In conclusion, monitoring and improving your SEO performance is vital for small business owners looking to establish a strong online presence. By utilizing tools like Google Analytics and Google Search Console, regularly updating your website with fresh and relevant content, engaging in social media marketing, optimizing for mobile devices, incorporating video content, and focusing on conversion rate optimization, you can effectively enhance your SEO performance and drive sustainable growth for your business.

Chapter 5: Content Marketing

Creating a Content Marketing Strategy

In today's digital landscape, having a well-defined content marketing strategy is essential for small business owners. With the rise of digital marketing, social media marketing, search engine optimization (SEO), content marketing, mobile marketing, video marketing, and conversion rate optimization, it is crucial to have a plan in place to effectively reach and engage your target audience. In this subchapter, we will explore the key steps involved in creating a content marketing strategy that drives results.

1. Define Your Goals: Before diving into content creation, it is important to identify your objectives. Are you looking to increase brand awareness, generate leads, or drive conversions? Understanding your goals will help you shape your content strategy accordingly.

2. Understand Your Target Audience: To create content that resonates with your audience, you must first understand who they are. Conduct market research, analyze your current customer base, and gather insights into their demographics, interests, and pain points. This information will guide you in crafting content that meets their needs and preferences.

3. Develop a Content Plan: A well-thought-out content plan outlines the types of content you will create, the channels you will use to distribute it, and the frequency of your content publication. Consider utilizing a mix of blog posts, videos, infographics, and social media content to keep your audience engaged across various platforms.

4. Create Engaging and Valuable Content: Your content should be informative, entertaining, and provide value to your audience. Use storytelling techniques, incorporate visuals, and ensure your content aligns with your brand voice and values. Remember, quality over quantity is key when it comes to content creation.

5. Optimize for Search Engines: Incorporate SEO techniques into your content to improve its visibility on search engines. Conduct keyword research, optimize your meta tags and headlines, and ensure your content is mobile-friendly. This will help drive organic traffic to your website and increase your online visibility.

6. Leverage Social Media: Social media platforms offer a great opportunity to distribute and promote your content. Identify the platforms where your target audience spends their time, create engaging social media posts, and utilize social media advertising to amplify your reach.

7. Measure and Analyze Results: Regularly monitor and analyze the performance of your content marketing efforts. Use analytics tools to track key metrics such as website traffic, engagement, and conversions. This data will provide insights into the effectiveness of your strategy and allow you to make informed decisions to optimize your content.

By following these steps and constantly refining your approach, you can create a content marketing strategy that not only increases your online presence but also drives tangible results for your small business. Remember, consistency, relevancy, and value are the pillars of a successful content marketing strategy.

Developing High-Quality and Relevant Content

In the increasingly digital world we live in, effective marketing strategies are essential for small business owners to stay competitive. One vital aspect of digital marketing is creating high-quality and relevant content that resonates with your target audience. In this subchapter, we will explore the key principles and strategies to develop content that engages, informs, and converts.

Digital Marketing: A Practical Guide for Small Business Owners is designed to equip you with the knowledge and skills necessary to navigate the complex world of digital marketing. Whether you are new to the field or looking to enhance your existing strategies, this subchapter will serve as a valuable resource.

Understanding the importance of content marketing is the first step towards success. By providing valuable and informative content, you can position yourself as an industry expert and build trust with your target audience. We will delve into the various types of content marketing, including blog posts, articles, videos, and social media posts, and explore how to tailor each to maximize engagement.

Search engine optimization (SEO) is another crucial component of content development. We will guide you through the process of optimizing your content to rank higher in search engine results, driving organic traffic to your website. From keyword research to on-page optimization, we will cover the essential SEO strategies that every small business owner should implement.

In today's digital landscape, social media marketing plays a pivotal role in reaching and engaging with your target audience. We will provide practical tips and techniques to leverage social media platforms effectively, including how to create compelling posts, engage followers, and measure the success of your social media campaigns.

Mobile marketing and video marketing are rapidly growing niches that cannot be ignored. We will explore the best practices for developing mobile-friendly content and creating engaging videos that captivate your audience. Additionally, we will discuss how to optimize your website and landing pages for mobile devices to ensure a seamless user experience.

Lastly, we will touch on conversion rate optimization (CRO), which focuses on turning website visitors into customers. By implementing CRO strategies, you can improve your website's performance and increase your conversion rates. We will provide practical tips on optimizing your landing pages, calls-to-action, and overall user experience.

In conclusion, developing high-quality and relevant content is at the core of any successful digital marketing strategy. By understanding the principles and strategies outlined in this subchapter, small business owners can create compelling content that drives engagement, increases brand awareness, and ultimately leads to business growth.

Content Distribution and Promotion

In today's digital age, creating high-quality content is just the first step towards success in the online world. To truly make an impact and reach your target audience, effective content distribution and promotion strategies are essential. This subchapter will delve into the various methods and techniques that small business owners can employ to maximize the visibility and reach of their content in the vast digital landscape.

Digital Marketing allows small business owners to leverage the power of the internet to promote their products and services. By utilizing various digital channels such as websites, social media platforms, search engines, and email marketing, businesses can target their audience more effectively and increase brand awareness. This subchapter will provide insights into the different digital marketing techniques that can be used to distribute and promote content, including social media marketing, search engine optimization (SEO), content marketing, mobile marketing, video marketing, and conversion rate optimization.

Social media marketing has become an integral part of digital marketing strategies. Platforms such as Facebook, Twitter, and Instagram offer businesses the opportunity to connect with their target audience, share content, and build brand loyalty. This subchapter will explore the best practices for social media marketing, including creating engaging content, utilizing hashtags, and leveraging influencers to reach a wider audience.

Search Engine Optimization (SEO) is another crucial aspect of content distribution and promotion. By optimizing your website and content for search engines, you can increase your visibility in search results and drive organic traffic to your website. This subchapter will delve into the key SEO techniques, such as keyword research, on-page optimization, and link building, that small business owners can implement to improve their search engine rankings.

Content marketing is all about creating valuable and relevant content that resonates with your target audience. This subchapter will provide insights into how small business owners can develop an effective content marketing strategy, including creating a content calendar, repurposing content for different platforms, and measuring the success of your content marketing efforts.

Mobile marketing and video marketing are two rapidly growing areas in the digital marketing landscape. With the majority of internet users accessing content through mobile devices and the increasing popularity of video content, small business owners need to adapt their distribution and promotion strategies accordingly. This subchapter will explore the best practices for mobile marketing and video marketing, including optimizing content for mobile devices, creating engaging video content, and utilizing video-sharing platforms like YouTube.

Conversion rate optimization is the process of improving the user experience on your website to drive more conversions, whether it be sales, sign-ups, or downloads. This subchapter will provide practical tips for optimizing your website's design, navigation, and call-to-action buttons to maximize conversions.

In conclusion, content distribution and promotion are vital components of any digital marketing strategy. By implementing the techniques and strategies outlined in this subchapter, small business owners can effectively distribute and promote their content, reach their target audience, and ultimately drive business growth.

Measuring Content Marketing Success

In today's digital landscape, content marketing has become an essential strategy for small business owners to reach and engage their target audience. However, the true success of content marketing lies in effectively measuring its impact and return on investment (ROI). In this subchapter, we will explore various metrics and tools that small business owners can use to measure the success of their content marketing efforts.

One of the key metrics to consider is website traffic. By monitoring your website's traffic, you can gauge the effectiveness of your content in attracting visitors. Tools like Google Analytics provide valuable insights into the number of visitors, their demographics, and the pages they visit most frequently. By analyzing this data, you can identify which content pieces are driving the most traffic and adjust your strategy accordingly.

Another important metric is engagement. This can be measured through social media metrics such as likes, comments, shares, and follows. By monitoring the engagement levels of your content, you can determine which pieces resonate the most with your audience and tailor future content to meet their needs and interests.

Furthermore, tracking conversions is crucial for assessing the effectiveness of your content marketing efforts. Conversions can be defined as the desired actions you want your audience to take, such as signing up for a newsletter, making a purchase, or requesting a quote. By implementing conversion tracking tools, such as Google Analytics' goal tracking feature, you can measure the conversion rate of your content and optimize it for better results.

Additionally, monitoring your search engine rankings can provide valuable insights into the success of your content marketing strategy. Tools like Moz and SEMrush allow you to track your website's position in search engine result pages (SERPs) for relevant keywords. By regularly tracking these rankings, you can identify trends, optimize your content for better visibility, and drive more organic traffic to your website.

In conclusion, measuring the success of your content marketing efforts is crucial for small business owners to optimize their strategies and achieve their marketing goals. By monitoring metrics such as website traffic, engagement, conversions, and search engine rankings, you can gain valuable insights into the effectiveness of your content and make data-driven decisions to enhance your digital marketing, social media marketing, search engine optimization (SEO), content marketing, mobile marketing, video marketing, and conversion rate optimization efforts.

Chapter 6: Mobile Marketing

Mobile Marketing Trends and Statistics

In today's digital world, mobile marketing has become an essential strategy for small business owners looking to reach and engage with their target audience. With the increasing use of smartphones and tablets, it is crucial to understand the latest trends and statistics in mobile marketing to stay ahead of the competition. This subchapter will provide valuable insights into the ever-evolving world of mobile marketing, helping small business owners navigate this dynamic landscape.

1. Mobile usage is on the rise: According to recent statistics, the number of mobile users worldwide is expected to reach 7.26 billion by 2023. This staggering figure highlights the immense potential of mobile marketing and the need for businesses to optimize their strategies for mobile devices.

2. Mobile-first indexing: Google's mobile-first indexing approach means that websites are now primarily ranked based on their mobile version rather than the desktop version. This shift emphasizes the importance of having a mobile-friendly website that offers a seamless user experience across all devices.

3. Mobile shopping is booming: E-commerce is experiencing a significant shift towards mobile devices. Studies show that 79% of smartphone users have made a purchase online using their mobile devices in the past six months. Small businesses need to optimize their websites for mobile shopping and ensure a user-friendly checkout process to capitalize on this trend.

4. Mobile advertising is effective: Mobile advertising offers an excellent opportunity for small businesses to reach their target audience. Research indicates that mobile ads have a higher click-through rate compared to desktop ads, making it a cost-effective marketing channel.

5. Rise of mobile video marketing: With the popularity of platforms like YouTube and TikTok, mobile video marketing has become an effective way to engage with customers. Small business owners can leverage video content to tell compelling stories, showcase products/services, and enhance brand awareness.

6. Mobile apps for customer engagement: Developing a mobile app can be a game-changer for small businesses. It allows for personalized experiences, push notifications, loyalty programs, and streamlined customer engagement, leading to increased customer satisfaction and brand loyalty.

7. SMS marketing for customer retention: SMS marketing continues to be an effective tool for small business owners to retain and engage customers. Sending personalized offers, updates, and reminders through SMS can help strengthen the customer relationship and drive repeat business.

As a small business owner, understanding these mobile marketing trends and statistics is vital for staying competitive in the digital landscape. Incorporating mobile marketing strategies into your overall digital marketing plan can lead to increased brand visibility, customer engagement, and ultimately, higher conversion rates. Embrace the power of mobile marketing to unlock new opportunities and grow your business in the digital age.

Responsive Website Design and Mobile Optimization

In today's digital age, having a strong online presence is crucial for small businesses to thrive. One of the key elements of a successful online strategy is a well-designed website that is optimized for mobile devices. In this subchapter, we will delve into the importance of responsive website design and mobile optimization, and how it can benefit small business owners in various digital marketing niches.

Responsive website design refers to the practice of creating websites that adapt and respond to different screen sizes and devices. With the increasing use of smartphones and tablets, it is essential for small business websites to be mobile-friendly. A responsive design ensures that your website looks and functions seamlessly across all devices, providing a positive user experience and increasing the chances of conversion.

Why is this important for small business owners? Let's consider the niches of digital marketing, social media marketing, search engine optimization (SEO), content marketing, mobile marketing, video marketing, and conversion rate optimization.

In digital marketing, a responsive website design is the foundation of your online presence. It allows you to effectively promote your business across various channels and devices, ensuring that potential customers have a consistent and engaging experience.

When it comes to social media marketing, a mobile-friendly website is crucial for driving traffic from social platforms. With a responsive design, your content can be easily shared and accessed on mobile devices, increasing brand visibility and engagement.

Search engine optimization (SEO) plays a vital role in driving organic traffic to your website. Search engines prioritize mobile-friendly websites in their rankings, making mobile optimization an essential aspect of SEO strategy for small business owners.

Content marketing relies on delivering valuable and engaging content to your audience. With a responsive website design, your content can be easily consumed on any device, allowing you to reach a wider audience and increase user engagement.

Mobile marketing, video marketing, and conversion rate optimization all benefit from responsive website design. A mobile-friendly website ensures that your marketing campaigns are accessible and effective on mobile devices, leading to higher conversion rates and customer satisfaction.

In conclusion, responsive website design and mobile optimization are essential for small business owners in the digital marketing landscape. By ensuring your website is mobile-friendly, you can effectively engage with your audience, drive traffic, improve search engine rankings, and ultimately increase conversions. Embracing responsive design will provide your small business with a strong online presence and a competitive edge in today's mobile-driven world.

Mobile Advertising and App Marketing

In today's digital age, mobile advertising and app marketing have become essential components of any successful marketing strategy. With the increasing use of smartphones and tablets, small business owners need to adapt to this mobile-centric world to effectively reach their target audience. This subchapter will provide small business owners with valuable insights into mobile advertising and app marketing, helping them leverage these powerful tools to grow their businesses.

Mobile advertising is the process of promoting products or services through mobile devices such as smartphones and tablets. With the majority of people spending a significant amount of their time on mobile devices, mobile advertising offers a unique opportunity to reach potential customers. From display ads to in-app advertisements, there are various formats available to small business owners to engage their target audience effectively.

App marketing focuses on promoting and driving app installations. As mobile apps continue to gain popularity, small business owners can leverage this platform to enhance customer engagement and boost brand loyalty. This subchapter will explore various app marketing strategies, including app store optimization, in-app advertising, and push notifications, enabling small business owners to effectively promote their apps and drive user acquisition.

To succeed in mobile advertising and app marketing, small business owners should consider the following best practices:

1. Mobile optimization: Ensure that your website and landing pages are optimized for mobile devices. Mobile users expect a seamless browsing experience, and a mobile-friendly website will help drive conversions.

2. Targeted advertising: Utilize mobile advertising platforms that offer advanced targeting options. This will allow you to reach your ideal customers based on demographics, interests, and behavior, maximizing the effectiveness of your ad campaigns.

3. App store optimization (ASO): Optimize your app's listing on app stores to improve its visibility and increase downloads. This includes optimizing the app title, description, keywords, and screenshots.

4. In-app advertising: Consider placing ads within popular mobile apps that align with your target audience. This form of advertising can be highly effective in reaching engaged users and driving app installations.

5. Push notifications: Utilize push notifications to engage with your app users and keep them informed about new products, offers, or updates. Personalized and timely push notifications can significantly improve user retention and drive conversions.

By understanding the power of mobile advertising and app marketing, small business owners can expand their reach, engage their target audience, and drive conversions. Integrating mobile advertising and app marketing into their overall digital marketing strategy will enable them to stay ahead of the competition and achieve their business goals.

Location-Based Marketing

In the ever-evolving world of digital marketing, one strategy that has gained significant traction in recent years is location-based marketing. With the increasing use of smartphones and the growing popularity of location-based services, small business owners have a unique opportunity to target their potential customers based on their geographical location. This subchapter will delve into the concept of location-based marketing, its benefits, and how small business owners can leverage this strategy to drive more foot traffic and boost their overall marketing efforts.

Location-based marketing, also known as geotargeting or geomarketing, involves delivering targeted advertising messages or promotions to individuals based on their physical location. This strategy utilizes technology such as GPS or IP address tracking to determine a user's location and deliver relevant content customized to their specific area. By leveraging this information, small business owners can create more personalized and targeted marketing campaigns that resonate with their local audience.

The benefits of location-based marketing are numerous. Firstly, it allows small business owners to reach customers precisely when they are in close proximity to their physical store or business location. This real-time targeting can significantly increase the chances of converting potential customers into actual buyers. Additionally, location-based marketing can help small business owners gain a competitive edge by providing relevant promotions or offers to customers who may be considering their competitors.

There are several ways small business owners can incorporate location-based marketing into their digital marketing strategies. Social media platforms, such as Facebook and Instagram, offer location-based advertising options that allow businesses to target users based on their current location or areas they frequently visit. By utilizing these tools, small business owners can reach potential customers who are most likely to be interested in their products or services.

Another effective method of location-based marketing is optimizing business listings on search engines and online directories. By ensuring that their business information is accurate, up-to-date, and optimized for local search queries, small business owners can increase their visibility in local search results and attract customers searching for products or services in their area.

Mobile marketing and video marketing also play a crucial role in location-based marketing. By creating mobile-friendly content and incorporating location-based targeting into mobile ads or videos, small business owners can engage with their local audience and drive them to take action, such as visiting their physical store or making a purchase online.

In conclusion, location-based marketing offers small business owners a powerful tool to connect with their target audience on a more personal and localized level. By leveraging the capabilities of digital marketing, social media marketing, search engine optimization (SEO), content marketing, mobile marketing, video marketing, and conversion rate optimization, small business owners can take advantage of the growing trend of location-based marketing to drive more foot traffic, boost sales, and enhance their overall marketing efforts.

Chapter 7: Video Marketing

Importance of Video Marketing in Digital Strategy

Video marketing has emerged as a powerful tool in the digital age, providing small business owners with a unique opportunity to engage and connect with their target audience. In an era where attention spans are diminishing, video content allows businesses to convey their message quickly and effectively. This subchapter will explore the significance of video marketing in a comprehensive digital strategy, highlighting its impact on various niches such as digital marketing, social media marketing, search engine optimization (SEO), content marketing, mobile marketing, and conversion rate optimization.

Digital Marketing:
Video marketing has become an integral part of digital marketing strategies. By incorporating videos into their campaigns, small business owners can enhance their brand visibility, attract more website traffic, and generate leads. Videos can be shared across multiple digital platforms, increasing the chances of reaching a wider audience and boosting brand awareness.

Social Media Marketing:
Social media platforms have become increasingly video-centric, with features such as Facebook Live, Instagram Stories, and TikTok dominating user engagement. Small businesses that leverage video marketing on these platforms can build a loyal following, increase user engagement, and drive conversions. By creating engaging and shareable video content, businesses can tap into the viral nature of social media and maximize their reach.

Search Engine Optimization (SEO):
Video content is highly favored by search engines, as it keeps users engaged for longer periods, leading to increased dwell time on websites. By optimizing video content with appropriate keywords, descriptions, and tags, small

businesses can improve their website's search engine rankings. Videos also have a higher chance of appearing in search engine results pages, giving businesses an added advantage in driving organic traffic.

Content Marketing:
Videos offer a dynamic and versatile medium for delivering valuable content to consumers. By creating informative, engaging, and entertaining videos, small businesses can establish themselves as industry experts and thought leaders. Video content can be repurposed across various platforms, such as blogs, social media, and email marketing, amplifying its reach and impact.

Mobile Marketing:
With the rise of mobile usage, videos have become a preferred form of content consumption on smartphones and tablets. Small businesses that prioritize video marketing can effectively target mobile users, creating visually appealing and easily accessible content that resonates with their audience.

Conversion Rate Optimization:
Videos have proven to be highly effective in driving conversions. By incorporating persuasive and compelling videos into their landing pages and sales funnels, small businesses can enhance their conversion rates. Videos can showcase product demonstrations, customer testimonials, and provide a personalized touch, ultimately influencing consumers' purchase decisions.

In conclusion, video marketing plays a crucial role in a comprehensive digital strategy for small businesses. By leveraging videos across various niches such as digital marketing, social media marketing, SEO, content marketing, mobile marketing, and conversion rate optimization, small business owners can effectively engage their target audience, boost brand visibility, and drive business growth in the digital landscape.

Creating Compelling Video Content

Video marketing has become an essential component of any successful digital marketing strategy. In this subchapter, we will explore the art of creating compelling video content that captivates your audience and drives engagement. Whether you are a small business owner venturing into the world of digital marketing, social media marketing, search engine optimization (SEO), content marketing, mobile marketing, or conversion rate optimization, incorporating video into your campaigns will help you effectively communicate your message and achieve your business goals.

First and foremost, it is crucial to understand your target audience and their preferences. Conduct market research to identify the demographics, interests, and behaviors of your audience. This will provide valuable insights into the type of videos that will resonate with them. For instance, if your target audience consists of tech-savvy millennials, short and visually appealing videos are likely to be more effective.

When creating video content, focus on storytelling. Craft a narrative that connects with your audience on an emotional level. Tell stories that evoke empathy, humor, or inspiration, as these tend to leave a lasting impact. Incorporate your brand's unique personality and values into the storyline, establishing a strong connection with your viewers.

Furthermore, keep your videos concise and to the point. In today's fast-paced world, attention spans are fleeting. Aim for videos that are no longer than two to three minutes, delivering your key message within the first few seconds to grab viewers' attention. Remember, the goal is to engage and retain your audience, so keep your content engaging and visually appealing throughout.

Invest in high-quality production, both in terms of visuals and audio. Poorly produced videos can reflect poorly on your brand image. Ensure your videos have a professional look and feel, with clear visuals and crisp audio. Additionally, consider incorporating subtitles or closed captions to cater to viewers who prefer watching videos without sound.

Lastly, optimize your videos for search engines. Develop a keyword strategy specific to video content and include relevant keywords in your video titles, descriptions, and tags. This will improve your video's visibility in search engine results and increase the likelihood of reaching your target audience.

In conclusion, creating compelling video content is essential for small business owners looking to excel in digital marketing, social media marketing, SEO, content marketing, mobile marketing, and conversion rate optimization. By understanding your audience, crafting engaging narratives, keeping videos concise, investing in high-quality production, and optimizing for search engines, you can create videos that leave a lasting impact and drive meaningful engagement with your target audience. Embrace the power of video marketing and elevate your digital presence to new heights.

Video Optimization for Search Engines

In today's digital landscape, it is becoming increasingly important for small business owners to leverage video marketing as part of their overall digital marketing strategy. With the rise of platforms like YouTube and the growing popularity of video content on social media, videos have become a powerful tool to attract and engage audiences. However, simply creating videos is not enough. To ensure that your videos are discoverable and rank well in search engine results, it is crucial to optimize them for search engines. This subchapter will provide you with practical tips and strategies to optimize your videos for search engines.

1. Keyword Research: Just like in traditional SEO, conducting keyword research is the first step in optimizing your videos. Identify relevant keywords and phrases that your target audience is likely to use when searching for content related to your business.

2. Video Title and Description: Optimize your video title and description by incorporating your target keywords naturally. Make sure the title accurately reflects the content of the video, and the description provides a concise summary of what viewers can expect.

3. Tags and Categories: Utilize relevant tags and categories to help search engines understand the context and subject matter of your video. This will improve the chances of your video appearing in related search results.

4. Thumbnail Optimization: Choose an eye-catching and relevant thumbnail image for your video. Thumbnails play a significant role in attracting viewers and enticing them to click on your video.

5. Transcriptions and Closed Captions: Including transcriptions and closed captions in your videos not only makes them more accessible to a wider audience but also provides search engines with text-based content that can be indexed. This enhances the discoverability of your videos.

6. Video Sitemaps: Creating a video sitemap and submitting it to search engines can improve your video's visibility in search results. A video sitemap provides search engines with valuable metadata about your videos, improving their chances of being indexed and ranked.

7. Embedding and Sharing: Encourage others to embed and share your videos on their websites and social media platforms. This increases the visibility and reach of your videos, ultimately improving their search engine rankings.

By implementing these video optimization techniques, you can enhance the visibility and reach of your videos in search engine results. This will not only drive more traffic to your website but also increase brand awareness and engagement with your target audience. Remember, video optimization is an ongoing process, so regularly monitor and analyze your video performance to make necessary adjustments and improvements.

Video Advertising and Promotion

In today's digital landscape, video advertising and promotion have become essential strategies for small business owners looking to stay ahead of the competition. With the rise of social media, search engine optimization (SEO), and mobile marketing, harnessing the power of video marketing has never been more important. In this subchapter, we will explore the benefits, best practices, and strategies for effectively using video to promote your business.

Video marketing offers a unique opportunity to engage and captivate your audience. With the ability to convey emotions, tell stories, and showcase your products or services, videos can create a lasting impact on potential customers. Moreover, incorporating videos in your digital marketing efforts can significantly improve your website's SEO, as search engines increasingly prioritize video content in their algorithms.

To leverage video advertising and promotion successfully, it is crucial to understand your target audience and tailor your content accordingly. Small business owners must identify the platforms their audience uses most frequently, whether it's social media channels like Facebook, Instagram, or YouTube. By creating videos optimized for these platforms, you can reach a wider audience and increase your chances of conversions.

When creating video content, it is essential to focus on quality and authenticity. Small business owners should strive to produce videos that reflect their brand's personality and values. Whether it's through behind-the-scenes footage, customer testimonials, or product demonstrations, authenticity will help your videos resonate with viewers and build trust.

Furthermore, optimizing your videos for mobile viewing is crucial, as mobile usage continues to increase year after year. Ensuring your videos are responsive and load quickly on mobile devices will enhance the user experience and increase the likelihood of engagement.

Conversion rate optimization is another key consideration when using video advertising and promotion. Small business owners should strategically place calls-to-action within their videos, encouraging viewers to take the desired action, such as making a purchase, signing up for a newsletter, or contacting the business. Additionally, tracking and analyzing video metrics will provide valuable insights into viewer behavior, allowing you to refine and optimize your video marketing strategy over time.

In conclusion, video advertising and promotion are indispensable tools in today's digital marketing landscape. By creating high-quality, authentic videos optimized for social media, SEO, and mobile devices, small business owners can effectively engage their target audience, increase brand awareness, and drive conversions. By incorporating video marketing into their overall digital marketing strategy, small business owners can stay ahead of the competition and thrive in the ever-evolving world of digital marketing.

Chapter 8: Conversion Rate Optimization

Understanding Conversion Rate and its Importance

In the ever-evolving digital landscape, small business owners need to have a deep understanding of various marketing strategies to stay ahead in the competitive market. One crucial aspect of digital marketing that demands attention is the conversion rate. This subchapter will delve into the concept of conversion rate and its immense importance in driving business growth.

Conversion rate refers to the percentage of website visitors who take a desired action, such as making a purchase, subscribing to a newsletter, or filling out a contact form. It is a key metric that allows small business owners to measure the effectiveness of their digital marketing efforts. By understanding the conversion rate, you can gauge the success of your campaigns and make data-driven decisions to optimize your marketing strategies.

For small business owners, understanding the importance of conversion rate is paramount. A high conversion rate means that your marketing efforts are resonating with your target audience and attracting customers to your business. It signifies that your website is user-friendly, your content is engaging, and your offers are compelling enough to convert visitors into paying customers. On the other hand, a low conversion rate indicates potential issues that need to be addressed, such as poor website design, confusing navigation, or ineffective calls-to-action.

Furthermore, a high conversion rate leads to increased revenue and business growth. By optimizing your conversion rate, you can generate more leads, increase sales, and ultimately boost your bottom line. It allows you to make the most out of your marketing budget by ensuring that every visitor to your website has a higher chance of becoming a customer.

To improve your conversion rate, it is crucial to implement various digital marketing strategies. These may include social media marketing, search engine optimization (SEO), content marketing, mobile marketing, video marketing, and conversion rate optimization (CRO). Each of these niches plays a significant role in attracting potential customers, engaging with them, and ultimately converting them into loyal patrons.

In conclusion, understanding conversion rate and its importance is essential for small business owners who want to thrive in the digital landscape. By measuring and optimizing your conversion rate, you can ensure that your marketing efforts are effective, generate more leads, and drive business growth. In the following chapters, we will explore each aspect of digital marketing and how it contributes to improving the conversion rate, providing you with practical strategies to implement in your small business.

Identifying Conversion Rate Optimization Opportunities

In the world of digital marketing, driving traffic to your website is only half the battle. The ultimate goal is to convert that traffic into paying customers. This is where Conversion Rate Optimization (CRO) comes into play. CRO is the process of improving the percentage of visitors who take a desired action on your website, such as making a purchase, signing up for a newsletter, or filling out a contact form.

As a small business owner, understanding and capitalizing on CRO opportunities is crucial for the success of your online marketing efforts. By optimizing your conversion rates, you can maximize the return on your investment and grow your business.

So how do you identify CRO opportunities? Here are some key areas to focus on:

1. User Experience (UX): Start by analyzing the overall user experience on your website. Is it easy to navigate? Are there any design flaws or technical issues that may hinder conversions? Conduct user testing and gather feedback to uncover any pain points and improve the overall usability of your site.

2. Landing Pages: Pay special attention to your landing pages, as they play a significant role in driving conversions. Analyze the performance of each landing page and identify areas for improvement. Test different headlines, call-to-action buttons, and content to see what resonates best with your audience.

3. Call-to-Actions (CTAs): Take a closer look at your CTAs across your website. Are they clear, compelling, and persuasive? Make sure they stand out and guide visitors towards the desired action. Consider using action-oriented language and incorporating urgency to prompt immediate action.

4. Forms and Checkout Process: If you have forms or an e-commerce checkout process on your website, streamline them to eliminate any unnecessary steps or barriers. Simplify the form fields, minimize the number of required fields, and ensure that the process is smooth and intuitive.

5. Content Optimization: Evaluate your website content and ensure that it is relevant, engaging, and tailored to your target audience. Use persuasive copywriting techniques to highlight the benefits of your products or services and address any objections or concerns your potential customers may have.

6. Analytics and Heatmaps: Utilize analytics tools and heatmaps to gain insights into user behavior on your website. Identify pages with high bounce rates or low engagement and investigate the reasons behind them. This data will help you make informed decisions on how to optimize those pages for better conversions.

By paying attention to these key areas, you can uncover valuable CRO opportunities and make data-driven changes that will enhance your website's performance. Remember, CRO is an ongoing process, so continuously monitor and test different strategies to improve your conversion rates.

In the next chapter, we will dive deeper into specific CRO techniques and tactics that you can implement to further boost your online conversions. Stay tuned!

A/B Testing and Conversion Rate Optimization Techniques

In the fast-paced world of digital marketing, staying ahead of the competition is crucial for small business owners. With the constant evolution of consumer behavior and preferences, it is essential to employ effective strategies that can maximize conversions and enhance overall business growth. This subchapter will delve into the concepts of A/B testing and conversion rate optimization techniques, empowering small business owners with the knowledge and tools they need to succeed in the digital landscape.

A/B testing is a powerful technique that allows businesses to compare two different versions of a webpage or marketing campaign to determine which one performs better. By testing various elements such as headlines, images, call-to-action buttons, or even the layout of a landing page, small business owners can gain valuable insights into what resonates with their target audience. This data-driven approach eliminates guesswork and enables businesses to make informed decisions based on real-time results.

Conversion rate optimization (CRO) is the process of improving the percentage of website visitors who take a desired action, such as making a purchase, filling out a form, or subscribing to a newsletter. By employing CRO techniques, small business owners can optimize their marketing efforts to maximize conversions and ultimately drive revenue. This subchapter will explore various CRO techniques, including persuasive copywriting, user-friendly website design, and effective call-to-action strategies.

For small business owners in the digital marketing niche, A/B testing and CRO are indispensable tools for success. By constantly experimenting and refining their marketing strategies, they can achieve higher conversion rates, increase customer engagement, and ultimately boost their bottom line. Additionally, this subchapter will address the specific challenges and opportunities presented by social media marketing, search engine optimization (SEO), content marketing, mobile marketing, video marketing, and conversion rate optimization.

In conclusion, A/B testing and conversion rate optimization techniques are essential for small business owners looking to thrive in the digital marketing landscape. By leveraging these strategies, they can make data-driven decisions, optimize their marketing efforts, and achieve higher conversion rates. This subchapter will provide small business owners in the digital marketing niche with a practical guide, equipping them with the necessary tools and knowledge to succeed in a competitive online environment.

Analyzing and Improving Conversion Funnel

In the fast-paced world of digital marketing, understanding and optimizing your conversion funnel is crucial to the success of your small business. The conversion funnel refers to the journey a potential customer takes from their initial interaction with your brand to making a purchase or completing a desired action. By analyzing and improving this funnel, you can identify areas for improvement and increase your conversion rates, ultimately driving more revenue for your business.

One of the first steps in analyzing your conversion funnel is tracking and measuring key metrics. This includes monitoring website traffic, click-through rates, bounce rates, and conversion rates at each stage of the funnel. By utilizing tools such as Google Analytics, you can gain valuable insights into how users are interacting with your website and where they may be dropping off.

Once you have identified potential bottlenecks in your funnel, it's time to start making improvements. One effective strategy is to optimize your website's user experience. Ensure that your website is visually appealing, easy to navigate, and mobile-friendly. A seamless user experience will encourage visitors to stay on your site longer and increase the likelihood of conversion.

Another essential aspect of improving your conversion funnel is creating compelling and relevant content. Content marketing plays a crucial role in engaging potential customers and guiding them through the funnel. By producing high-quality blog posts, videos, and social media content, you can establish your brand as an expert in your niche and build trust with your audience.

Furthermore, leveraging the power of social media marketing and search engine optimization (SEO) is essential to driving traffic to your website and increasing conversions. By optimizing your website for relevant keywords and implementing a solid social media strategy, you can attract qualified leads and guide them through the conversion funnel.

Mobile marketing and video marketing are also crucial components of a successful conversion funnel. With the increasing use of mobile devices and the popularity of video content, it's essential to ensure your website is mobile-friendly and create engaging video content to capture your audience's attention.

Lastly, conversion rate optimization (CRO) techniques can help fine-tune your funnel and maximize your conversion rates. A/B testing, heat mapping, and user feedback surveys can provide valuable insights into user behavior and help identify areas for improvement.

By analyzing and improving your conversion funnel, you can optimize your digital marketing efforts and drive more revenue for your small business. Implementing these strategies and continuously monitoring and adjusting your funnel will ensure you stay ahead of the competition and achieve long-term success in the digital landscape.

Chapter 9: Measuring and Analyzing Digital Marketing Performance

Key Metrics for Measuring Digital Marketing Performance

In the ever-evolving world of digital marketing, it is crucial for small business owners to have a clear understanding of the key metrics that can help measure the success of their marketing efforts. By tracking these metrics, you can gain valuable insights into the effectiveness of your digital marketing strategies and make data-driven decisions to optimize your campaigns. In this subchapter, we will explore the key metrics for measuring digital marketing performance across various niches, including digital marketing, social media marketing, search engine optimization (SEO), content marketing, mobile marketing, video marketing, and conversion rate optimization.

Digital Marketing Metrics:

1. Return on Investment (ROI): This metric measures the profitability of your digital marketing campaigns by comparing the revenue generated to the cost of your marketing efforts.

2. Cost per Acquisition (CPA): CPA calculates the average cost of acquiring a customer through your digital marketing channels. It helps determine the effectiveness and efficiency of your marketing campaigns.

Social Media Marketing Metrics:

1. Engagement Rate: This metric measures the level of interaction and involvement your audience has with your social media content, such as likes, comments, shares, and clicks.

2. Reach: Reach measures the number of unique users who have seen your social media content. It helps gauge the potential impact of your social media campaigns.

SEO Metrics:

1. Organic Traffic: Organic traffic refers to the number of visitors coming to your website through search engine results. Tracking organic traffic helps evaluate the success of your SEO efforts.

2. Keyword Rankings: Monitoring your website's rankings for targeted keywords on search engine results pages (SERPs) is essential to measure the effectiveness of your SEO strategies.

Content Marketing Metrics:

1. Engagement Metrics: These metrics include time spent on page, bounce rate, and scroll depth. They provide insights into how engaging and valuable your content is to your audience.

2. Conversion Rate: Conversion rate measures the percentage of visitors who take a desired action on your website, such as making a purchase or filling out a form. It helps determine the effectiveness of your content in driving conversions.

Mobile Marketing Metrics:

1. App Downloads: If you have a mobile app for your business, tracking the number of app downloads can help measure its popularity and success.

2. App Engagement: Metrics like session duration, daily active users, and retention rate help measure how engaged your app users are and the overall success of your mobile marketing efforts.

Video Marketing Metrics:

1. View Count: The number of views your videos receive is a key metric to measure the reach and popularity of your video marketing campaigns.

2. Engagement Metrics: These include likes, comments, shares, and click-through rates. They help determine how well your videos resonate with your audience.

Conversion Rate Optimization Metrics:

1. Conversion Rate: This metric measures the percentage of website visitors who complete a desired action, such as making a purchase. It helps evaluate the effectiveness of your optimization efforts.

2. A/B Testing Results: A/B testing allows you to compare two versions of a webpage or an element to determine which performs better in terms of conversions. Tracking the results helps optimize your website for better conversion rates.

By focusing on these key metrics, small business owners can gain valuable insights into the performance of their digital marketing efforts and make informed decisions to improve their marketing strategies. Remember, measuring and analyzing these metrics regularly is crucial to staying ahead in the digital marketing landscape and achieving sustainable growth for your business.

Using Google Analytics for Tracking and Reporting

In this digital age, tracking and analyzing data is crucial for the success of any small business. With the advancement of technology and the rise of online marketing, it has become increasingly important to understand your audience's behavior and make data-driven decisions. One powerful tool that can help you achieve this is Google Analytics.

Google Analytics is a free web analytics platform that provides valuable insights into your website's performance, user behavior, and conversion rates. It offers a wide range of features that can help you understand how your digital marketing efforts are performing, including social media marketing, search engine optimization (SEO), content marketing, mobile marketing, video marketing, and conversion rate optimization.

When it comes to digital marketing, having a strong online presence is vital. Google Analytics allows you to track your website's traffic sources, such as organic search, social media referrals, or paid advertisements. This information can help you determine which channels are driving the most traffic to your website, allowing you to allocate your marketing budget effectively.

Furthermore, Google Analytics provides detailed insights into user behavior on your website. You can track how users navigate through your site, which pages they visit the most, and how long they stay on each page. This data is invaluable for optimizing your website's user experience and identifying areas for improvement.

For small businesses investing in SEO, Google Analytics is an essential tool. It allows you to track your organic search traffic, monitor keyword rankings, and analyze the effectiveness of your SEO strategies. By identifying the keywords that drive the most traffic and conversions, you can refine your SEO efforts and rank higher in search engine results.

Content marketing is another key aspect of digital marketing, and Google Analytics can help you measure its impact. You can track the performance of your blog posts, videos, and other content assets, including the number of views, engagement metrics, and conversion rates. This data can guide your content strategy and ensure that you are producing valuable and engaging content for your target audience.

Mobile marketing has become increasingly important as more people use their smartphones to browse the internet. Google Analytics provides insights into your mobile traffic, allowing you to optimize your website for mobile devices and tailor your marketing campaigns accordingly.

Finally, Google Analytics can help you measure the success of your conversion rate optimization efforts. By setting up goals and tracking conversions, you can identify which pages or marketing campaigns are driving the most conversions, and optimize them for better results.

In conclusion, Google Analytics is an indispensable tool for small business owners in the digital marketing space. It provides valuable insights into various aspects of your online presence, helping you make data-driven decisions and optimize your marketing efforts. By leveraging the power of Google Analytics, you can stay ahead of the competition and achieve greater success in the digital realm.

Interpretation of Data and Making Data-Driven Decisions

In today's digital age, data has become the lifeblood of successful marketing campaigns. As a small business owner, it is crucial to understand how to interpret data and make data-driven decisions to maximize the effectiveness of your digital marketing strategies. This subchapter will provide you with valuable insights on how to harness the power of data across various aspects of digital marketing.

Digital Marketing:
Data analysis plays a pivotal role in digital marketing. By closely monitoring key metrics such as website traffic, click-through rates, and conversion rates, you can gain valuable insights into the effectiveness of your marketing efforts.

These insights can help you identify areas for improvement, optimize your campaigns, and allocate resources more efficiently.

Social Media Marketing:
Social media platforms provide a wealth of data that can be used to drive your marketing decisions. By analyzing engagement metrics such as likes, shares, and comments, you can measure the impact of your social media campaigns. This data can inform your content strategy, target audience selection, and even the timing of your posts, ensuring that you reach and engage your target customers effectively.

Search Engine Optimization (SEO):
Data analysis is essential for optimizing your website's SEO. By analyzing keyword rankings, organic search traffic, and user behavior on your site, you can identify high-performing keywords, optimize your website content, and improve your search engine rankings. Data-driven SEO decisions can help you attract more organic traffic, increase visibility, and ultimately generate more leads and sales.

Content Marketing:
Data-driven decisions can greatly enhance your content marketing efforts. By analyzing metrics such as engagement, time on page, and conversion rates, you can identify the type of content that resonates most with your target audience. This data can guide your content creation process, ensuring that you deliver valuable and relevant content that drives results.

Mobile Marketing:
With the majority of consumers accessing the internet through mobile devices, data analysis is crucial in optimizing your mobile marketing strategies. By analyzing mobile traffic patterns, bounce rates, and conversion rates, you can tailor your mobile campaigns to provide a seamless user experience and drive higher conversion rates.

Video Marketing:
Data plays a vital role in measuring the success of your video marketing campaigns. By analyzing metrics such as views, watch time, and engagement, you can gauge the effectiveness of your videos and make data-driven decisions on content, distribution channels, and targeting. This will help you create compelling videos that resonate with your audience and achieve your marketing objectives.

Conversion Rate Optimization:
Data analysis is paramount in improving your conversion rates. By analyzing user behavior, conducting A/B tests, and tracking conversion funnels, you can identify areas where users drop off and make data-driven decisions to optimize your website or landing page. This can significantly improve your conversion rates and maximize the return on your marketing investments.

In conclusion, interpreting data and making data-driven decisions are essential skills for small business owners in the digital marketing realm. By harnessing the power of data across various digital marketing niches, you can optimize your strategies, reach your target audience more effectively, and drive better results for your business.

Chapter 10: Implementing and Managing Digital Marketing Campaigns

Creating an Effective Campaign Execution Plan

As a small business owner, you understand the importance of digital marketing and its potential to drive growth and success. However, without a well-thought-out campaign execution plan, your efforts may fall flat. In this subchapter, we will explore the key steps to creating an effective campaign execution plan, ensuring that you maximize your digital marketing efforts across various channels, including social media marketing, search engine optimization (SEO), content marketing, mobile marketing, video marketing, and conversion rate optimization.

1. Set Clear Goals: Before diving into any campaign, it is crucial to define your objectives. Are you looking to increase brand awareness, generate leads, drive website traffic, or boost sales? By clearly defining your goals, you can align your campaign strategies accordingly.

2. Understand Your Target Audience: To create an effective campaign, you must have a deep understanding of your target audience. Conduct thorough market research to identify their needs, preferences, and pain points. This will help you tailor your messages and content to resonate with your audience, increasing the likelihood of engagement and conversion.

3. Develop a Comprehensive Content Strategy: Content lies at the heart of any successful digital marketing campaign. Create a content strategy that aligns with your goals and target audience. Determine the types of content that will resonate with your audience, such as blog posts, videos, infographics, or

podcasts. Develop a content calendar to ensure consistency and plan content distribution across various channels.

4. Optimize for Search Engines: Implementing effective SEO strategies is crucial to improving your website's visibility and driving organic traffic. Conduct keyword research to identify relevant keywords and incorporate them naturally into your website's content. Optimize meta tags, headings, and URLs to improve your website's search engine rankings.

5. Leverage Social Media: Social media platforms provide an excellent opportunity to connect with your audience, increase brand awareness, and drive traffic to your website. Identify the most relevant platforms for your business and develop a social media strategy that aligns with your goals. Create engaging content, interact with your audience, and leverage social media advertising to reach a wider audience.

6. Embrace Mobile Marketing: With the significant increase in mobile device usage, optimizing your campaigns for mobile is vital. Ensure that your website is mobile-friendly and responsive. Leverage SMS marketing, mobile advertising, and location-based marketing to reach your target audience on their smartphones.

7. Utilize Video Marketing: Videos have become a powerful tool in digital marketing. Create engaging and informative videos that showcase your products or services, provide tutorials, or share customer success stories. Leverage platforms like YouTube, Instagram, or TikTok to reach your audience and drive engagement.

8. Continuously Monitor and Optimize: To ensure the success of your campaigns, it is essential to monitor their performance regularly. Analyze key metrics like website traffic, conversion rates, engagement, and ROI. Based on the insights, make necessary adjustments and optimizations to improve campaign effectiveness.

By following these key steps and implementing an effective campaign execution plan, you can maximize your digital marketing efforts across various channels. Stay up-to-date with the latest trends and technologies in digital marketing to continuously refine and improve your campaigns, enabling your small business to thrive in the digital landscape.

Managing Digital Marketing Campaigns Effectively

In today's digital age, small business owners have an array of powerful tools at their disposal to reach and engage with their target audience. Digital marketing has become an indispensable strategy for growing businesses, providing a cost-effective way to promote products and services, increase brand visibility, and drive sales. However, without proper management, these campaigns can quickly become overwhelming and ineffective. This subchapter aims to equip small business owners with the knowledge and skills necessary to manage their digital marketing campaigns effectively.

First and foremost, it is crucial to develop a comprehensive digital marketing strategy. This strategy should outline the business's goals, target audience, and key performance indicators (KPIs) to track success. By understanding the desired outcomes, small business owners can tailor their campaigns accordingly. Additionally, this strategy should include an analysis of the competition, market trends, and customer insights to gain a competitive edge.

One of the primary components of successful digital marketing campaigns is social media marketing. Platforms such as Facebook, Instagram, Twitter, and LinkedIn enable businesses to connect directly with their target audience, build relationships, and drive traffic to their websites. By utilizing analytics tools, small business owners can track the effectiveness of their social media efforts and make data-driven decisions to optimize their campaigns.

Search engine optimization (SEO) is another critical aspect of managing digital marketing campaigns effectively. By optimizing their websites and content for search engines, small business owners can increase organic visibility and drive targeted traffic. This subchapter will provide practical tips on keyword research, on-page optimization, link building, and monitoring SEO performance.

Moreover, content marketing plays a vital role in engaging and nurturing potential customers. By creating valuable and relevant content, small business owners can establish themselves as industry experts and build trust with their audience. This subchapter will delve into various content marketing techniques, including blogging, email marketing, and guest posting.

With the rise of mobile devices, small business owners must also consider mobile marketing strategies. Mobile-friendly websites, SMS marketing, and mobile apps are just a few examples of how businesses can tap into the mobile market effectively. The subchapter will explore the best practices for mobile marketing and provide insights on how to optimize campaigns for mobile users.

Video marketing is another powerful tool for small business owners to engage their audience. With platforms like YouTube and TikTok gaining immense popularity, businesses can leverage video content to tell their brand story, demonstrate product features, and connect with their target audience emotionally. This subchapter will offer guidance on creating compelling video content and optimizing its distribution.

Lastly, managing digital marketing campaigns effectively requires a focus on conversion rate optimization (CRO). By analyzing user behavior, conducting A/B testing, and refining landing pages, small business owners can improve their conversion rates and maximize their return on investment. This subchapter will provide practical tips on CRO techniques and tools.

In conclusion, managing digital marketing campaigns effectively is essential for small business owners to thrive in today's competitive landscape. By developing a comprehensive strategy, utilizing social media, SEO, content marketing, mobile marketing, video marketing, and conversion rate optimization, businesses can reach their target audience, build brand awareness, and drive growth. This subchapter serves as a practical guide for small business owners to navigate the digital marketing realm successfully.

Monitoring and Adjusting Campaign Performance

In the fast-paced world of digital marketing, it is crucial for small business owners to constantly monitor and adjust their campaigns to ensure maximum effectiveness and return on investment. This subchapter explores the importance of monitoring and adjusting campaign performance across various digital marketing niches, including social media marketing, search engine optimization (SEO), content marketing, mobile marketing, video marketing, and conversion rate optimization.

In the realm of social media marketing, monitoring campaign performance involves tracking key metrics such as engagement rate, click-through rate, and reach. By regularly analyzing these metrics, small business owners can identify which social media platforms and content types are resonating with their target audience. Adjustments can then be made to optimize campaigns, such as reallocating resources to platforms that deliver the best results or refining content strategies to better engage followers.

Similarly, search engine optimization (SEO) campaigns require careful monitoring and adjustment to improve search engine rankings and drive organic traffic. Tracking metrics like keyword rankings, organic traffic, and bounce rates can provide valuable insights into the effectiveness of SEO efforts. Adjustments may involve optimizing on-page content, building quality backlinks, or refining keyword strategies to better align with user intent.

Content marketing campaigns also benefit from regular monitoring and adjustment. By analyzing metrics such as website traffic, time spent on page, and conversion rates, small business owners can determine which types of content are generating the most engagement and driving conversions. Adjustments may involve creating more of the high-performing content, repurposing content for different platforms, or refining the content strategy to better address customer pain points.

For small business owners delving into mobile marketing and video marketing, monitoring campaign performance is essential to ensure optimal user experience and engagement. Metrics such as app downloads, mobile website traffic, video views, and completion rates can reveal valuable insights about audience preferences and behavior. Adjustments may involve optimizing mobile websites for better performance, creating shorter and more engaging videos, or targeting specific demographics with tailored mobile ads.

Lastly, conversion rate optimization (CRO) focuses on monitoring and adjusting campaign performance to improve the percentage of website visitors who take desired actions. By analyzing metrics like conversion rates, bounce rates, and click-through rates, small business owners can identify areas of improvement in their sales funnels. Adjustments may involve A/B testing different landing pages, simplifying the checkout process, or improving call-to-action buttons.

In conclusion, monitoring and adjusting campaign performance is vital for small business owners in the ever-evolving digital marketing landscape. By closely tracking key metrics and making necessary adjustments, entrepreneurs can optimize their digital marketing efforts across various niches, ultimately driving better results and growing their businesses.

Chapter 11: Future Trends in Digital Marketing

Emerging Technologies and their Impact on Digital Marketing

In today's rapidly evolving digital landscape, staying ahead of emerging technologies is crucial for small business owners looking to succeed in the competitive world of digital marketing. As new technologies continue to shape consumer behavior and expectations, it is essential to understand their impact and harness their potential to drive business growth. In this subchapter, we will explore some of the most important emerging technologies and how they influence various aspects of digital marketing.

1. Artificial Intelligence (AI) and Machine Learning: AI and machine learning algorithms have become increasingly sophisticated, enabling businesses to automate and optimize various marketing processes. From chatbots that engage with customers in real-time to personalized product recommendations, AI is revolutionizing customer experiences and driving conversions.

2. Virtual and Augmented Reality (VR/AR): VR and AR technologies offer unique opportunities for small businesses to engage with their target audience in immersive and interactive ways. Whether it's showcasing products in virtual showrooms or allowing customers to try on virtual clothing, VR and AR can enhance brand experiences, increase engagement, and drive sales.

3. Voice Search and Smart Speakers: With the rise of voice assistants like Siri, Alexa, and Google Assistant, voice search has become an integral part of consumers' daily lives. Optimizing your digital marketing strategies for voice search can help improve search engine rankings and increase brand visibility in this rapidly growing segment.

4. Blockchain Technology: While commonly associated with cryptocurrencies, blockchain technology has the potential to revolutionize digital marketing by providing secure and transparent transactions. It can enhance trust between businesses and customers, especially in industries like e-commerce, by verifying the authenticity of products and protecting sensitive data.

5. Internet of Things (IoT): IoT devices are becoming increasingly prevalent, connecting various elements of our lives, from smart homes to wearable devices. Leveraging IoT data can help small businesses gain valuable insights into customer behavior and preferences, enabling them to deliver personalized marketing messages and experiences.

6. Data Analytics and Predictive Modeling: Advanced data analytics tools and predictive modeling techniques allow small businesses to make data-driven decisions and create highly targeted marketing campaigns. By analyzing large volumes of data, businesses can identify trends, predict customer behavior, and optimize marketing efforts for maximum impact.

As a small business owner, it is vital to stay informed about these emerging technologies and understand how they can be leveraged to boost your digital marketing efforts. While implementing every technology may not be feasible, identifying the ones that align with your business goals and target audience can give you a competitive edge in the dynamic digital landscape.

Remember, digital marketing is an ever-evolving field, and staying abreast of emerging technologies will help you adapt to changing consumer behaviors, enhance your marketing strategies, and ultimately drive business growth.

Predicting and Adapting to Future Trends

In the ever-evolving world of digital marketing, staying ahead of the curve is crucial for small business owners like you. Understanding and adapting to future trends can give you a competitive edge and help you make informed decisions when it comes to your digital marketing strategy. In this subchapter, we will explore the importance of predicting and adapting to future trends in various digital marketing niches such as social media marketing, search engine optimization (SEO), content marketing, mobile marketing, video marketing, and conversion rate optimization.

Social media marketing has become an integral part of any successful digital marketing strategy. However, the landscape is constantly changing, with new platforms and features emerging regularly. Predicting future trends in social media can help you identify which platforms to focus on and how to engage with your target audience effectively. By staying up-to-date with the latest trends and adapting your social media strategy accordingly, you can ensure maximum reach and engagement.

Search engine optimization (SEO) is a fundamental aspect of digital marketing, as it determines how easily your website can be found by potential customers. As search engines continuously update their algorithms, predicting and adapting to future trends in SEO is essential for maintaining high search rankings. Keeping an eye on emerging SEO techniques and optimizing your website accordingly can help you stay ahead in search engine results pages and drive organic traffic to your website.

Content marketing plays a vital role in establishing your brand's authority and attracting and retaining customers. By predicting future trends in content marketing, you can create valuable and engaging content that resonates with your target audience. Adapting to these trends, such as the rise of video content or the increasing importance of interactive content, can help you stay relevant and maintain a strong content marketing strategy.

Mobile marketing is another rapidly growing niche in digital marketing. With the increasing use of smartphones and mobile devices, predicting and adapting to future trends in mobile marketing is crucial for reaching your target audience effectively. This can include optimizing your website for mobile devices, creating mobile-friendly ads, and exploring new mobile marketing channels.

Video marketing has become extremely popular in recent years, and its importance is only expected to grow. Predicting and adapting to future trends in video marketing can help you create compelling video content that captures your audience's attention. This can include exploring new video platforms, such as TikTok or Instagram Reels, and experimenting with different video formats and storytelling techniques.

Finally, conversion rate optimization focuses on maximizing the number of website visitors who take desired actions, such as making a purchase or filling out a contact form. By predicting and adapting to future trends in conversion rate optimization, you can optimize your website's user experience, experiment with new conversion tactics, and improve your overall conversion rates.

In conclusion, predicting and adapting to future trends in digital marketing is essential for small business owners. By staying informed about the latest trends and adapting your strategies accordingly, you can stay ahead of the competition and ensure the success of your digital marketing efforts in the ever-evolving digital landscape.

Chapter 12: Conclusion

Recap of Key Digital Marketing Strategies

In this subchapter, we will provide a comprehensive recap of some key digital marketing strategies that every small business owner should be aware of. As the digital landscape continues to evolve rapidly, it is crucial to stay updated on the latest techniques and trends to effectively promote your business online. Whether you are new to digital marketing or seeking a refresher, this recap will help you understand the core strategies in various niches, including digital marketing, social media marketing, search engine optimization (SEO), content marketing, mobile marketing, video marketing, and conversion rate optimization.

Digital Marketing:
Digital marketing encompasses all online marketing efforts to promote products or services. It involves a combination of strategies such as search engine marketing, email marketing, social media marketing, and content marketing, among others. The goal is to reach and engage with a target audience, drive traffic to your website, and convert leads into customers.

Social Media Marketing:
Social media marketing leverages social media platforms to connect with your target audience, build brand awareness, and drive website traffic. Strategies include creating engaging content, fostering online communities, and utilizing paid advertising to reach a wider audience.

Search Engine Optimization (SEO):
SEO is the process of optimizing your website to increase visibility on search engine result pages. This involves optimizing your website's structure, keywords, and content to rank higher in organic search results. Key strategies include on-page optimization, link building, and ensuring a mobile-friendly website.

Content Marketing:
Content marketing focuses on creating and distributing valuable, relevant, and consistent content to attract and retain a target audience. This can include blog posts, videos, infographics, and more. The goal is to establish your business as a trusted authority and drive customer engagement.

Mobile Marketing:
Mobile marketing targets users on mobile devices, such as smartphones and tablets. Strategies include mobile advertising, responsive website design, and mobile apps to engage with customers on the go.

Video Marketing:
Video marketing involves creating and promoting video content to engage with your audience. This can include product demonstrations, tutorials, testimonials, and behind-the-scenes footage. Video marketing has gained significant popularity due to its ability to convey messages more effectively and drive higher engagement.

Conversion Rate Optimization:
Conversion rate optimization focuses on improving the percentage of website visitors who take desired actions, such as making a purchase or filling out a form. Strategies include A/B testing, optimizing website design and user experience, and analyzing data to identify areas for improvement.

As a small business owner, understanding and implementing these key digital marketing strategies will help you effectively promote your business, reach your target audience, and achieve your marketing goals. Stay tuned for the following chapters, where we will dive deeper into each strategy, providing practical tips and best practices to help you succeed in the digital marketing realm.

Final Thoughts and Tips for Small Business Owners

Congratulations! You have reached the end of this practical guide for small business owners, and by now, you should have a good understanding of the key aspects of digital marketing. Before we wrap up, here are some final thoughts and tips to help you excel in the ever-evolving digital landscape.

Digital Marketing:
Digital marketing is not a one-time effort; it requires continuous learning and adaptation. Stay updated with the latest trends, tools, and strategies by attending conferences, webinars, and reading industry blogs. Embrace experimentation and be willing to try new approaches to find what works best for your business.

Social Media Marketing:
Social media has become an integral part of our lives, and it's essential for small businesses to leverage its power. Focus on building a strong social media presence by creating valuable, engaging content that resonates with your target audience. Encourage user-generated content and interact with your followers to build genuine relationships.

Search Engine Optimization (SEO):
SEO is crucial for increasing your website's visibility on search engines. Conduct keyword research and optimize your website's content, meta tags, and URLs accordingly. Build quality backlinks and ensure your website is mobile-friendly. Regularly monitor your website's performance using analytics tools and make necessary adjustments.

Content Marketing:
Content is king, and creating high-quality, relevant content is essential for attracting and retaining customers. Develop a content strategy that aligns with your business goals and target audience. Use a mix of formats, such as blog

posts, videos, infographics, and podcasts, to keep your content diverse and engaging.

Mobile Marketing:
With the rise of smartphones, mobile marketing has become a necessity. Optimize your website and emails for mobile devices, create mobile-specific ads, and consider developing a mobile app if it aligns with your business objectives. Personalize your mobile marketing efforts to provide a seamless user experience.

Video Marketing:
Video is a powerful tool for engaging your audience and conveying your brand story. Create compelling videos that educate, entertain, or inspire your viewers. Use platforms like YouTube and social media channels to share your videos and measure their performance through analytics.

Conversion Rate Optimization:
Increasing your website's conversion rate is crucial for maximizing your digital marketing efforts. Continuously test and optimize your website's design, layout, and calls-to-action to improve conversions. Analyze user behavior through heatmaps and user recordings to identify areas of improvement.

In conclusion, digital marketing offers immense opportunities for small businesses to grow and thrive. By investing time and effort into understanding and implementing the strategies discussed in this book, you can elevate your digital marketing game and stay ahead of the competition. Remember, success in digital marketing comes with continuous learning, adaptation, and experimentation. Good luck on your digital marketing journey!

www.ingramcontent.com/pod-product-compliance
Lightning Source LLC
Chambersburg PA
CBHW071101290526
45795CB00004B/1602